April's poems are fierce, fearless and ambitious. They're full of images that surprise me every time I read them and lines which jangle my spine. She conjures a world in which figures wear their "shed skin / as a blindfold", therapists "graverob out mindfulness activities" and "pain is a nuclear wallpaper". April's is a voice with incisive claws and iridescent wings: I'm so glad to have stood alongside her as it hatches and very excited to see where it flies.

— *Caleb Parkin*

Having grown up in a working-class, mixed-heritage British and Caribbean household, Kaycee Hill's influences range from hip-hop artists such as Floetry and Sade to lyric poets Sylvia Plath and John Keats. An urban voyeur, she brings the environmental attentiveness of eco-poetry to inner-city life and landscapes: from parks to prisons to the inside of a care home during the pandemic. Kaycee's writing is notable for its linguistic innovation, creative imagery and depth of emotion. Her innate talent is matched by the suppleness and precision of her craft – this is a killer combination and indicates great promise for the future.

— *Aviva Dautch*

'I laugh because oh my god, I've gone mad. I've started speaking to you, / to a fucking seagull.' Eve's writing is crisp, striking, and uniquely resonant. They use language that is both grounded and multi-faceted while exploring timely and necessary themes about class, mental health, and loneliness. A poet of poise and power. One to watch.

— *Romalyn Ante*

I0158589

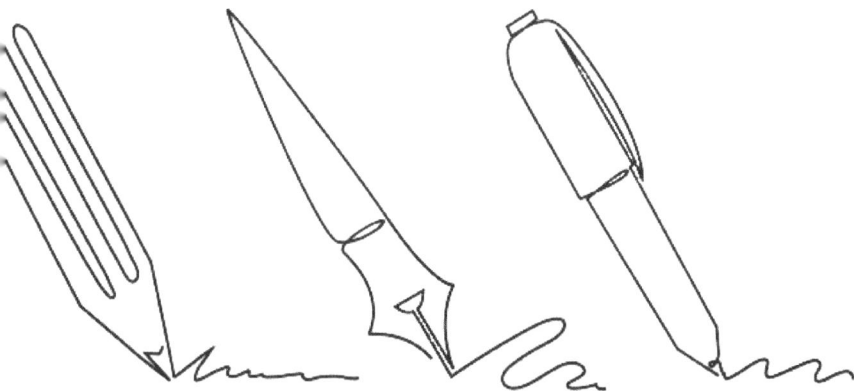

Poetry Ambassadors is a programme sponsored by the Winchester Poetry Festival in partnership with ArtfulScribe and the University of Southampton, thanks to generous support from The Foyle Foundation, Arts Council England, and the Arts and Humanities Research Council. The partners are grateful to Caleb Parkin, Romalyn Ante, and Aviva Dautch for their insight, expertise and care in mentoring April, Eve, and Kaycee during 2021, culminating in the production of this work.

POETRY AMBASSADORS

Egan, Hill, Wright

ISBN: 978-1-915079-98-5

Cover design by Aaron Kent

Typeset by Aaron Kent

Broken Sleep Books (2021)

Broken Sleep Books Ltd
Rhydwen,
Talgarreg,
SA44 4HB
Wales

Contents

Poetry Ambassadors

April Egan, Kaycee Hill, Eve Wright

April Egan

Mentored by:
Caleb Parkin

Biography

April is a poet and artist living on the Isle of Wight after spending her childhood as a migrant to Australia. She is a commended Foyle Young Poet and was also commended in the Orwell Youth Prize in 2020. Active on Young Poets Network, April's poetry revolves around identity and especially in the facets of queerness and lack of nationality. She is preparing to attend Cambridge in October, and having put together an award winning zine on an iPhone 4, now feels she can do anything.

upon the night's starred face

I fall in love with a tapeworm,
a waxing gas rag, cloudily

mewling for a crumb, a crust
of sun;

when you come home, I'll be
eating turf. you cry, &

it raises its wasted head for worship.

when you come home, I'll
be on my hands and knees with

hunger.

a papery resurrection, the wake
of flat ghosts, pill babies, girl oil

rumbles of silver milk-light vomit.

when you come home to our
organic cell

wearing your shed skin
as a blindfold, I will wear mine

thick as a shroud. we'll lie

rattling spoons

in the mouth of two slime moons

keeping,

eating each other whole.

'Why don't you tell me what the problem is?'

ten therapists in four years have asked,
     some begged.   they aren't getting it out of me

until they join me in the air, until those little paper cubes
     tick themselves back into the earth.   I wish
 I was beautifully ill

like a vanward cloud. but I'm its rider, an acrid cowboy.
I wish
     I was in love in the next poem,   not winking
through the latest

  flirtation with my memory -   when I float down
inkily to its lips,

    I disintegrate entirely, and wake up alone.
the therapist draws in sharply, puts their clipboard down.

you're not getting it out of me.

my first love told me I was blue, this is my least favourite
colour.
     and I told her so, instead of I love you too.

this is what I think of when they suck their teeth
     and graverob out mindfulness activities,

my mouth cleaves only bones and plastic oranges.
     you need to help yourself.

brain rimmed in fly traps, toothed hemisphere

     jammed sun,

would you like to touch me,

knowing all I can consume?

jawbone axis, sprawled syllable,

skating, choking, percolating.

you're not getting it out of me.

Success Hill

'I have my whole life to go the movies'
- The Babysitter's Club, 1995

the cowboys come home quiet having burnt down the hotel,
their thank-yous pressed in *babysitter's clubs,* rows and rows
of stacey's secret sugar tongue, mary-ann's dark hair burn-
ing through knee high socks, my disgusting clothes, my
rotting body bedroom

some other gross child will smell through the empty gym
disco
and all with our fingers wound in the chicken wire behind
the kindergarten   *claudia and the sad good-bye*
go to prom together in red rock ribbons   claudia cringes
when it kisses her forehead

and then the babysitter's ill   and I'm on success hill, and it's
thirty-seven degrees in the morning   VCR lysergic
heads tipped   split wide open   chewing on photo thread
      here   in the groin of the world   you   wyoming fresh

oh I'm nothin'
                                I'm nowhere…

please close the eyes in my neck   please put me on your
horse   and kookaburra me   our flat unmoving mouths   our
northern railways   rattling chainlink rainbows   it hurts to
speak in hills   so ride through the suburbs like a troubling
wind   an american girl fiddles with the bookmarks of the
darkness   like my head on your

torn back   favourite sons come here to be born   and they
ride in early to die   fists dunked in beer and licked by inci-
sors   maybe true love is two smokers with their heads in the
possibility   that this could grow and this is
        probably going to kill them

if you wake up in the witching hour, somebody's watching
you

somebody's lifting you   mallory stars and stripes the
night time wall with *I hate boys* while I tune the words pain-
fully high   on you   wild spokeshave   silver spur in orbit
jewellery   blood nose
        rags   dust-fucked   everyone's gone   you're never
coming back   I'm manic and needle-thighed   puncturing
perth's spine   as it holds me like currency
        take me away   lean down from your horse
and say something about mexico
        or sleeping on your feet   or heading north

and take me away   into the darkness
    where I watch myself sleep

I love you

                    and it's too hot
and it's too early   & god my eyes are in spasm

        half a dark blue
forty degree
                            vein
giddying
        far away
    I'm   nothing

                            I'm nowhere

pyotr illyich

A cut up based on 'The Cossacks' by Leo Tolstoy

dented touch,

become a handful of plums,

a high gregorian ceiling that shakes
when they collide with pillars
hooking lips to semicolons

smeared pink. a voyeuristic snowflake on the debutantes
beribboned, shiny as bandaged tongues

before the wars, fans of fluttering light.

if you are a syllable of thread trapped in his scarf, you knot
forever at
bonsoir called clumsily over the frozen lake

the hands of an assassin, two-smiled,
mazurka with you gently before the naked fire, the sharp
cuticle of an epaulet as he holds his face,

steeling mantilla,
the thin lacy breath that hovers.

veil of a musket thrown in the grass,

catch yourself on the drummer boy's nail,
the smiles stepping on each other's toes, tumbling

home. the smoky stems of muscovite grass, a woman's
whisper, *you've grown taller. have some tea.*

you, the way a man sits with his head on his knees, caught in

the high, cringing sun of tenderness, the sound of arms hit-
ting flanks, you

the stately tree where he hides from bare skin.

and when the family gathers,
head to head, shawl to rapt attention, become a chandelier of
faces

burning forever.

Nuke Town, NA

someone called me a fag today
I didn't say because we're too happy,
pasteurised primary smiles hang on big pink walls,
bitten lips, America's teeth

it's always Christmas
in a burning yard, it's always summertime
when you wake up in half a life

shaking your fist at the huge lights & the choke & the
bloody BLOODY noise
here, because we're so happy, we sit in sunglasses indoors,
we go on strange trips

for the vibrato of fear, we see California foaming at the
mouth
jagged and rabid and living and dead

we come home as perfume and oxygen
kissing in front of the news static, all the blinds drawn.

because we're so happy,

this is the room of glow and swell and glow and swell
of my honey & I hate you & I just
can't live without you

because we're so happy here.

where your fork slips out of your hand,
and the ceiling caves in, the air goes bust

quaking mire swatches across mean earth

pain is a nuclear wallpaper

our walls are an ingrown canyon.

the key to life as the last of your kind

when peace shrinks into the zeroes, cliffs sour
and we burn homework on the beach, punching smoke.
tourists abandoned all four chambers of the chalk heart
and left straggling cells, misshapen children's voices
short and sharp, tumbling over rocks and into the sea, lost
forever.

what stays is the antediluvian hush:
the bleary sick sound when seagulls put *slimming world* to
death, seaside games tremor forlornly, masked mouths caress
doorways, policemen inform them
that they *aren't* dead yet, not yet.

the key is willing it all to be evil, this crust is cold and thick
with evidence, a varicose breath
drowned and sucked clean, muddy splinters peel from the exit
when I'm washing my dead head in the fire
trying to fossilise,

the thin juncture of love stirs. I push it deep through the sand.
the new snowdrops force the heating off, the boys find a
dinosaur tooth in the woods,
gently wrap it in their shirts,
and tell me to close my eyes.

Kaycee Hill

Mentored by:
Aviva Dautch

Biography

Kaycee is a poet, creative writing graduate, and digital mixed media artist based in Southampton. Her poem *Scuffing* was performed and published on The British Museum's YouTube for Refugee Week 2021, The Poetry of Witness: writing about displacement, migration and exile. She was a shortlisted poet for the 2020 Poetry London Mentoring Scheme and commended for her poetry by The Young Poets Network. Kaycee defines herself as an urban voyeur, with much of her urge to write taken from the fidgeting mundanity of inner-city life.

Scuffing
after Maya Angelou

I picture my mother at eleven years old –

    bowlegged, pint-sized, confined in her uniform,
eyes weary even then, pulled in at the corners,
        cast in hickory, flecked with gold,

    the same shade Diana Ross and The Supremes wore
on the cover of *Cream of the Crop*, shook those hips in,

gappy teeth, freckled cheeks, walking home from school,
dragging new Clarks against salmagundi brick,

their leather-cracked cry trailing behind
    like the music of a cabassa made from gourd,
like bay leaves laughing, rice and peas boiling.

I see her enjoying the scuffing, reveling in its wrongness –

the desecration of shoes so foreign, so hideous,
    her mouth flung open to the sky like Maya's,
armed to the back teeth with glee

(that pot of Kiwi black polish under the sink, that'll slide over
the damage like shea butter).

    We need much less than we think we need
        did Mum consider that?

Did a guilt-seed bloom, nestled between mince roly-poly,
    mash and veg, coiling like bantu knots?

I see her playing out the trouble she'd be in, hearing it
    like an echo in an aluminum can,
        great-nanny's voice rearing up

over the ruins, the crime scene,

    then simmering down to a tiny puff of steam
because she's eleven, grown, a God –

Day Visit at HMP Erlestoke

We're ninety minutes into our voyage
          and everything is melting:
lamp posts, car-wheels, golden arches,
          glossy liquorice wires cuffing the sky,
cut between gums of cloud like dental floss,
a decrepit old village police station
          whose sign affirms L I E,
pot-bellied bins and flies,
cyclists in hi-vis and red-numbered cows
herded onto the clipped green,
          nervously awaiting a downpour.
          One droplet falls on my eye,
                    my pupil reflected in the window
                    inside a soup of motion
          where the world and everything in it
          has coalesced into this unknowable,
                    unsayable grey void –
                    then he surfaces,
          past the jangle of cables,
          lights and uniforms.
It's just our family left.
Awkward silence.
A single hug.
          Curious, isn't it,
how we come to find our inheritance
          whittled in skin?
          Driving away, Corinne Bailey Rae's
                    Girl Put Your Record On
                              crawls over the backseat,
                    gnaws on something deep.
                              Folkloric.
It settles in my eardrums like rain-spittle,
          like someone else's story.

To Get Inside

First, Mum gets out my birth certificate:
a strange fragment slid out of lilac plastic,

delicate as Great-Nanny's forearm flesh
and exclaiming in faded Britannia-red ink

every inch of my undeveloped history,
edges curdling under a slab of October sky

as if pained by this newfound nudity,
snatched by the tall lady's weighty hands.

Next zips un-zipped, pockets turned over,
gutted, contents laid out like a mass burial

across the nail-gouged laminated table.
Then down, to the menagerie of men,

to air clogged with cheap washing powder
and apple cider vinegar, the meaty balm

of Y chromosomes, and sound convulsing,
coagulating, into a brief, desperate hum.

Blessed

Over breakfast the Devil came to me,
belching sulphur all over my porridge.
Big bristled hooves, forked tongue,
three blinding breasts – heavy, round,
the shade of koff candy twists.

She offered me a one-eyed lamb's head,
tight-lipped clam shells, a box of tampons.
Her nipples cracked into a map
of Southampton, leaked honey,
melted the cutlery.

She squeezed the flaming teat in an antique
goblet, mixed it with tears then slid it
across the table – *drink me* – etched
into its base. She tasted sweet
like girlhood,

peppered with a musk I had tasted before:
my first experience with death
when Play died, finding unused needles
buried inside window ledges,
red inside white cotton,

smeared up the middle like roadkill.
Her flavour frenzied every bud,
like ants spewing wings, taking flight.
I felt one hundred hymens breaking
like bird skulls,

tumescence of hips swelling to the ocean,
the smell of Golden Virginia,
baked tarmac, lemon Shake n' Vac,
taste of Parma Violets, crayons,
microwaved milk.

Through this mirage I saw mountains
of bubblegum taffeta, clear princess
tiara gems, Anne Frank's diary –
dog eared, hair stuffed into Bic razors
and my first big-girl bedroom.

Care Bears stood to attention on entry,
all white tummies, fat and full.
And my old rocking horse restored
to glory, exactly how I kept her,
with the bridle removed,

a box stood in the nucleus of the room,
inside it smelt like pencil shavings, lilies,
stay here forever, the Devil said –
brushing my hair with one coiled paw,
as the goblet topped itself up.

I took a sip, kneaded into her lap
and let sleep take me,

locusts fell from her cheeks,

the sun laboured a look.

Earth's Human Shores
after John Keats

My mother's brown lifelines track across
the sand of her palms, languidly joining
like barking gulls in the place where
secrets are formed or the wind speaks.

There's a face – a woman's, a graveyard
of trees or nipples pointing to Hades
dozing her stomach like roasted papayas,
and a map with clear rivers, their shells

softly turning, just to feel the sun close.
This place is ancient as comb-jelly –
where the spawning ground dances
with ideas in new combinations:

a waltz for mourning, snaking hips at war
or the mambo in love. Excavate the clag,
the clart. Make a bright star from stone
and from the mountains and the moors.

Push yourself into the valley of ghosts.
It's like the moon cracking herself open.
It's like jiving bees. A woman in the shape
of a beast, a beast in the shape of a woman.

Our Faces

I soak the flannel, wipe over
        the salt caves of sleep clutched
                in your eyes' inner corners,

        you hate this part the most –
when light is temporarily banished.

I understand the helplessness,
        why you shake with fear
                until the world sets into focus.

You laugh as I hold out my hands,
        my blue plastic-wrapped fingers,

        and try a few aimless notes,
vowels bouncing all around us,

        a mirage of floating faces
                reflected in white tile.

You look over me
        with your small ripe eyes
                and those endless black pupils,

        creased lids pulsing
like you're trying to say something.

        I'm listening – I'm listening –
but I'm still unable to decode the message

and you cup your wilting hands
        into ramekins,
                one for each of us,

as if to say: I know you see me
               I see you too

Eve Wright

Mentored by:
Romalyn Ante

Biography

Eve is an autistic and queer writer/poet currently based in Poole. They were a commended Foyle Young Poet of the Year in 2020, and have been commissioned as part of the BBC New Creatives scheme* for their audio piece *Anchor*. They are very grateful to have been published in Ambit, but still can't quite believe it. They will be studying Biomedical Science at Portsmouth this upcoming October and politely ask that you don't tell anyone they are in fact a mad scientist in disguise.

*A talent development scheme for writers and artists supported by Arts Council England and BBC Arts, delivered in the South West by Calling The Shots.

Dying at Poole Park

1

Did you know? The sun was so bright it could melt the ice.
The M2 buses come every five minutes, a college rush-hour lie.
So we walk through the park because it's quicker.
He knows it is. He knows everything – that boy,
and I wish he didn't because I was finally good at something.

2

He doesn't even fucking live around here,
he lives in Bearwood. He knows the park like the back of his hand.
I've been here since I was four and I'm still scared of dogs
and the swans in the pond —

did you know? They found a man in Poole Park.
Dead, apparently, all over the Daily Echo.
Some poor dog walker found them, or some runner.
We joke about why someone would get up and go for a run
when we contemplate skipping 9 am Physics
for ten minutes extra sleep.

3

The boy that knows everything
says he knows exactly where they found him.
In the undergrowth by the ice rink, third bush along on the left.
And when you can point out the exact location of a dead body
with such flushed jest, for a moment I wonder if he's alright.
He goes to CAMHS, so probably not. But I'm probably not either.
So, we talk about what happened to him and drugs come up,
like it's normal to wake up and overdose on heroin or codeine,
or something. Needles and tablets in the bushes.
My dad in place of the dead man
and I want to be sick.

4

Did you know? We started talking about clothes
and how they never fucking fit; why do they always change the sizes
in each shop you go into? The girl I dreamt about kissing on the bus once
mentions size zero and says they're made for anorexics. I'm not,
I'm just shaped like a stick,
but I look at her like I am. She apologises and she probably means it.
But who means anything they say in times like these?

5

Did you know? We talk about what buses we are getting
and I say the number 8, back to the council estate.
They scoff, turn noses up, like they all do, when the weed
catches at the back of the throat. They catapult
shit at the buses, don't they? Rocks, eggs,
or something. They paint the entire neighbourhood black.

We're all fucking thugs here, good for nothings, sex and kids
at sixteen, no GCSEs. But hey, the girl I dreamt about kissing
on the bus once, says I'm not like them, I'm alright. But —

6

I laugh because oh my god, I've gone mad. I've started speaking to you,
to a fucking seagull. You have to laugh at that, don't you?
At the crazy things we do to console ourselves in times like these.

Did you know? Sometimes I want to die
or run away, or both.

7

Did you know? We found you dead.
You looked like a fountain ornament at first,
erected in the greenery by the crazy golf. But
we got closer and your guts were spewing
like a fountain spewing water. I jump and they laugh
because I jump, and I laugh because I have to fit in.
But all I can see is your intestines as my noose.
I thought I was better than this, but I guess not. They laugh
because they can't believe that for a second I believed
you were something beautiful; cast in porcelain
like a Greek god, wings shattering from the fall away of grace.

A sonnet for my grandmother

"To live in hearts we leave behind is not to die."
— *Thomas Campbell*

How I wish I knew the language of love,
how to splinter the moon to get to you.
And how I wish I knew the skin and the rough
that memory hides in; the fingertips they fall through.

How I wish I knew the language of a spectre,
how to fit your voice in the shape of their mouth.
And how I wish I knew the connector
of grief — a scarred soul, a body buried south.

How I wish I knew the language of an empty room,
how to make quiet something worth dying for.
And how I wish I knew the hug of your womb
so I could cling to all the lives you lived before.

How I wish I knew the language of home,
how to rebuild you when there's nothing left but bone.

Blackberry

They calcified into thorns every summer,
metastasized blackberries like tumours.

A soft, surgical removal within tissue
under the anesthetic warmth of June.

In the half sleep, the remission, the wintertide
pain ripened. Made you cry.

They insisted it isn't back again, fed you antibiotics,
but those thorns scratched you still.

At your funeral, Dancing Queen haunts the air.
There is no rain. Grief is raw, the sun stings.

After the memorial, we walk through the gardens
A final goodbye told in cheese sandwiches, scones

spilling jam. I poke holes in the leftover picnic boxes,
hoping for a single thread of light to bleed through.

Chasing Ghosts

There are years of mutual anguish in the
you are worth it tattooed onto the peeling
fence guarding the White Cliffs of Dover.
Two people stand on the edge of the cliff

and carve their undying love into the rocks.
A child's encouragement chalked into the paving
is pure and bright and sure of itself. *Keep going!*
My feet walk tired crop circles around

the fine line between giving up and letting go.
The heat makes the water turn into sunburnt lemonade
and I leave shortbread crumbs in hopes of finding myself
as we wade through the field towards the main road;

my Converse blue and rusted in a ghost of green.
The flowers grow in impossible places—
tree roots, cracks of pavements, through
the soles of my grandmother's feet.

My phone thinks I'm in France for five minutes
and in that time I drift and don't think about dying.
Friday's rain comes and the bluebirds hide under
the veranda, singing in symbiotic grief.

Napping is in the genes and not a "behavioral choice"

"No one ever told me that grief felt so like fear."
— C.S. Lewis

Scientists discovered
grief is turning all the lights out.

There's 123 regions in the human genome
telling us to indulge grief, shut the curtains.

They identified three potential napping mechanisms
sleep to remember a loved one
        to hold a loved one
            to escape a loved one.

I woke up at the crack of dawn
but all the clocks are half-asleep,
and my grandmother is already gone.

How much sleep is required by a particular individual
to visit the afterlife? I sleep more.

Napping gene variants were associated with orexin
proteins that fold like a blanket, my need to see her face once more.

The findings were published
in the order of service, a life well loved.

Some people nap more than others
I pretend she is still alive,
I pretend she never lived at all.

Findings from the British Medical Journal
suggest that acceptance is possible in the face of grief.
e.g. I wash my face and my acne sets
like a scabbed sun. Perhaps light will shine through.

According to the study,
there is a long way to go.

An ode to green

Mary Jane, she taught me the love language
of rolling a spliff perfectly between the fingers.
Psychedelic centrepieces on the coffee table,
a water fountain, a bird feeder. My feet crunch
under codeine stones that lead to my father,
one quicksilver cloud trying hard not to rain.
My father is ruining the garden. Or am I?
Recovery is the evergreen that would've survived
if it grew in a garden from the next town over.
My father said if anyone ever tells you
happiness doesn't come from trees, fuck 'em.
Perhaps I should not hold grudges against the way
a council house and its tenants learn to appreciate
their greenery and their nests. It is learned behaviour.
A father bird regurgitates food to satisfy his chick.
The spliff is an offshoot.

Acknowledgements

APRIL EGAN:

Thank you to Caleb Parkin, deeply and confidently, for the exceptional guidance and kindness across this poetic trek. Franz and I could never be more grateful. Thank you Liev Dorian, Stas Nikolai, Kristian Marian and Alba for the overflow, the sun and for letting me meet you here again. Thank you Hurst poets for your endless understanding and the awe you always leave me in. Laughing in the road we shall stay. Thank you very, very much to twelve year old April, who lived through it. It got better than you could ever imagine and especially thanks to Young Poets Network, who changed my life completely. And thank you most of all to Penelope Malcomson, who taught me everything I know about reading and writing.

KAYCEE HILL:

Thank you to all the mentors I've had over the years, official, invisible, and somewhere in-between, who have armed me to the back teeth with tools to apply language to my creative expression. Thank you to Mum and Dad for raising me on poetry outside of the canon. Thank you, Tyrone, for being my walking inspiration, I love you more than I could ever express on paper. Thank you to my soul sisters Jessica, Leah and Daisy, who have never wavered in supporting this dream of mine. Thank you, The British Museum, who kindly allowed me to have 'Scuffing' enjoyed on a huge platform, and to Aviva Dautch for curating it. Aviva, thank you for going above and beyond to push me to my poetic limits, for challenging me like no one else has and for making this journey exceptional, through workshops that have redefined my writing, my world, and my place in it. I couldn't have dreamt up a better mentor. And massive thanks to the Poetry Ambassadors Scheme, Artful Scribe, Broken Sleep Books and everyone involved, for ensuring that emerging voices are heard during a time when countless were stifled – from the bottom of my heart, thank you.

Eve Wright:

Thank you to *Ambit,* who kindly published "Dying at Poole Park" before it ended up here. And thanks to The Guardian for publishing the article that I pinched the title and some clauses from to write my poem "Napping is in the genes and not a "behavioural choice". Thank you Aaron and everyone at Broken Sleep Books, who have worked tirelessly to get this anthology to print. Your efforts do not go unnoticed. Kindest and most grateful thanks to all those that brought the Poetry Ambassadors scheme to life, in particular Romalyn Ante for giving up her time and reams of poetry knowledge to nurture my creations and push them to places I never believed possible, making my first ever mentoring opportunity an undoubtedly positive growing experience. Many thanks also to Aviva Dautch and Caleb Parkin for giving up their time and creativity to deliver wonderfully thought provoking workshops. Thank you to ArtfulScribe for their endless dedication in cultivating spaces for writers to come together, and all of their behind the scenes work to make them happen. I owe plenty of heartfelt thanks to Lighthouse Young Writers — without them, my writing may have never found itself, and I may have never found poetry and the countless opportunities that have come with it. Thank you especially to Tabby Hayward, who has answered every email, and read/listened to every piece of my work that I have offered up with bounds of enthusiasm, kindness and support. To all the neurodivergent writers out there trying to find their voice, I see you. To Cerys, my best friend, whom I promised I would shout out in my first published work. I am shouting you out with great pride. To my late nana Dot — I'll wave this anthology around up to the sky and risk being a lunatic; I hope you'll see it. And last but not least, a very sarcastic thanks to 2020 — you helped with my writers block, but I don't want to see you again.

LAY OUT YOUR UNREST